T0380963

MILLE LACS MONSTERS:
ONE MANS QUEST
TO CATCH THEM

MICHAEL WEHKING AND MATT TRENO

ISBN: Softcover   978-1-9845-2564-2
         Hardcover   978-1-9845-2565-9
         EBook   978-1-9845-2563-5

Print information available on the last page

Rev. date: 05/02/2018

To order additional copies of this book, contact:
Xlibris
1-888-795-4274
www.Xlibris.com
Orders@Xlibris.com

INTRODUCTION

They lurk near moss-covered shoreline rocks, by cattail-waving bays, and on sand and gravel flats laced with four-foot waves in areas known to few. They are the Mille Lacs monsters, huge fish known as muskie, walleye, and smallmouth. They are so big that state records will soon fall. One local fishing guide is stalking them—daily.

Meet Matt Treno, a salty tell-it-like-it-is Mille Lacs fishing guide with so many stories and photos of prized catches. He felt it was finally time to share his story, a story of a ten-year veteran guide who rose from poverty to prosperity in Mille Lacs fishing guide circles.

Having fished the lake since childhood, Treno has caught more walleyes, muskies, and smallmouth than the average area launch captain has dreamed about. He's won weekend tournaments and a fishing league, guided pros, and participated in the World Walleye Championships. He's even written some children's books.

A lanky, mildly graying, ponytail-sporting, flip-flop-wearing, cigarette-smoking seasoned angler, Treno knows his prey. He's up on the latest lures, baits, electronics, poles, and techniques. Like an army sniper, he stalks these Mille Lacs mammoths, proclaiming that one day Minnesota State records will be his alone.

He's probably not far off. He's got credentials. He's driven launches for the lake's best resorts, fished day and night, and can boast guiding more hopeful fishermen on the Big Pond than anybody I know. Big is an understatement for the 132,000-acre Mille Lacs Lake, a bowl-shaped body of water that is ranked the number 1 smallmouth fishery in North America.

The walleye ranking has slid a bit in recent times, as it was a victim of zebra mussels, netting during the spawn, Eurasian milfoil, and less agricultural runoff, which means clearer water and a host of less-understood miniplagues. None of this has stunted Treno's quest to land epic fish—the biggest fish Minnesota has ever produced!

In the ensuing five chapters, Treno tells his stories, shares anecdotes and techniques, and celebrates his many wins and few defeats. It's all there for you to see, touch, and almost smell. Like how the myriad fishing trails on his various GPS screens look like a Spirograph from the '70s, Treno's odyssey runs far and wide, stretching the full seventy-eight miles around Minnesota's most notorious *big* fish lake.

Now let's get to it!

CHAPTER 1

Treno's Start on Mille Lacs

Mille Lacs is Minnesota's second-largest lake. It's over 207 square miles and 132,000 acres. It sports muskies, walleyes, Northern, perch, tullibee, panfish, crappies, and rough fish, as well as countless loons, ducks, geese, and critters galore.

It's nestled across parts of four counties—Mille Lacs, Kanabec, Aitkin, and Crow Wing. It's been said that on a busy summer fishing weekend, more than 5,500 boats may be on the water, making it the biggest population center in East Central Minnesota.

Settled by various Indian tribes dating back to the 1700s, the Mille Lacs Band of Ojibwe have their reservation on the northwest shore, dominated by Grand Casino Mille Lacs. The lake is known to the Ojibwe as Misizaaga'gan (Grand/Great/Big Lake in the Region of a Thousand Lakes). It is the largest lake in the Brainerd Lakes Area.

I have lived on the south shore of the lake, at Izatys Resort, since 2005 and first met Matt Treno in the summer of 2007. You could hear him coming. His dirty old white Ford F-250 with a mismatched older red tailgate and bar a muffler would rumble down Par 5 Drive on the way to the marina, which is next to my front door. He would quickly back his trailered boat into the launch area, lower his skeeter into the water, and cruise to the main lake in a matter of minutes.

Matt would always wave, visit with marina gatekeeper Marlene Kruger, and share information about where he was catching fish. He's a happy, gregarious guy with a penchant for storytelling and having a couple of adult beverages when he's done fishing.

But Treno's start on the Big Pond goes way back!

CHAPTER 2

Lunkers

Those that fish in Mille Lacs know that today it could be home to state record muskies, walleyes, and smallmouth bass. It's got structure, habitat, and enough forage to produce monster fish.

In the last several years, Mille Lacs has produced near records in all these species.

That means besting the following Minnesota State records:

- An 8-pound smallmouth that dates back to 1948 on Battle Lake
- A 56-inch muskie weighing 54 pounds that dates back to 1957 on Lake Winnibigoshish
- A creature 34.5-inch, 21.25-pound walleye off the Seagull River in 1979

Some things we know as fact. The DNR annual creel surveys have told us much.

Every year, there are 31-inch walleyes caught on Mille Lacs. The other two species records—muskie and smallmouth—likely lurk in the lake today.

At least, Treno and a bevy of his followers and fellow guides think so.

Here are a couple of nice muskies Treno boated!

CHAPTER 3

A Couple of Days in the Life of Fishing Guide Matt Treno

My eyes open slowly. It's morning. I can see the light of day just pressing through the darkness outside. Stretching slowly in bed, I know my day is about to begin. After I rise to a sitting position, my morning duties begin. Today is going to be a good day!

Mornings start off simple. Checking weather and wind reports, I see our weather pattern is holding. It's the end of June, and our summer is in full swing here at Mille Lacs Lake. Winds are calm, and the weather is on tap for an amazing day.

When I'm done getting dressed (shorts, UV long-sleeved shirt, and of course, flip flops), my activities move to the kitchen area. I have breakfast while checking emails and the schedule for today's customers. Today's clients are from the Illinois area and are here looking to catch some smallies and maybe a few walleyes at dark. Our trip for the day isn't scheduled to start until the afternoon, so my morning is full of prep time.

Prep time is a very broad statement. This includes all kinds of things, like trips to the store, bank, and post office; getting gas for trucks and the boat; rod and reel repair; tackle prep; trips to the local tackle shops—the seemingly endless battle of projects that need to be done onshore. I hate shore time in the summer! After all the years of daily activities on the great waters of Mille Lacs, it's hard to be away, even for just a morning.

Moving forward, I meet with my customers (a group of two, a father and an adult son). They're excited, and we are off to the boat ramp. Ramp time is a time for many calculated movements and departures. This streamlined process is made simple by those of us here on our daily routines. For others, the boat ramp can be an adventure of trials and a lot of errors! I keep to myself and take care of my job at hand. I get my gear and the customers all loaded up, and off we go!

The weather is amazing! A slight breeze blows on the lake, enough to keep the bugs away and the air temps comfortable. There are a few boats around; it's Friday, and the weekend crowd is just starting to arrive. There are ducks off in the distance, and a man and his dog are playing with a ball at the house next to the ramp. One boat is backing into the lake, while another idles at the dock, waiting. The anticipation of all involved is high. We idle away from the dock; the trip has begun.

Our day starts off like most. It is a couple of miles' boat ride to our first fishing location while we take in the sights of the lake coming out of Cove Bay—trees, docks, fishermen, a couple of kayakers paddling across the bay. As we are passing through the channel into the main lake, a fisherman in a boat sets the hook as we drive by.

The younger of my two clients points to his father, and they nod in agreement. Arriving at our first location, I take the time to pass out equipment and explain our first tactics of the day. I also explain the location, bottom makeup, and things to look for. This first spot is a meet-and-greet spot. Ideally, I would look for a location where we can bend the rods, catch some fish, and get to know each other and where the clients can get used to my gear and tactics. The first spot will often set the tone for the rest of the day, so it's important to start strong.

This particular day is like most others. There is nothing huge at our first location, but we put three fish in the boat and miss a couple of others. The dad is struggling a bit with a couple of tactics; however, we get him dialed in, and he smacks his first bass of the day right before we move. There are pictures and some slimy high fives, and we are off!

The rest of the afternoon goes according to plan. We hop from spot to spot around the southwest side of Mille Lacs. We pull up to a location and discuss it and the presentations we'll use. We catch a fish or two, sometimes smallies and sometimes huge walleyes.

We continue this pattern till about dinnertime, when the boys decide to take a break and eat. I suggest we drop a couple of live bait rigs in and take a break. Of course, we land a couple of walleyes during sandwich/story time. Net man, fish weigher, picture taker, boat driver, line retying/rigging man, spot specialist, electronics expert, fishing advice giver, storyteller, and of course, a good listener / silent observer—these are all roles I have played on this trip so far. It is just another normal day.

With our bellies full and our hands still itching for more, we switch species to the elusive walleye (turns out those fish we caught while eating dinner are kind of fun). The sun is now dropping closer to the horizon. The lake has become calm and almost glasslike. I prepare the boat and its occupants for a longer ride. I turn to my customers and say, "Let's go on a boat ride." Now these words have meaning, and some of you that have fished with me have probably heard me mumble these words a time or two. This means we're switching gears. It's my way of mentally blocking what we were and have been doing to focus on what we are about to do. It also just signals that we are about to go on a longer-than-normal boat ride, sometimes just a mile or two, but often more like seven.

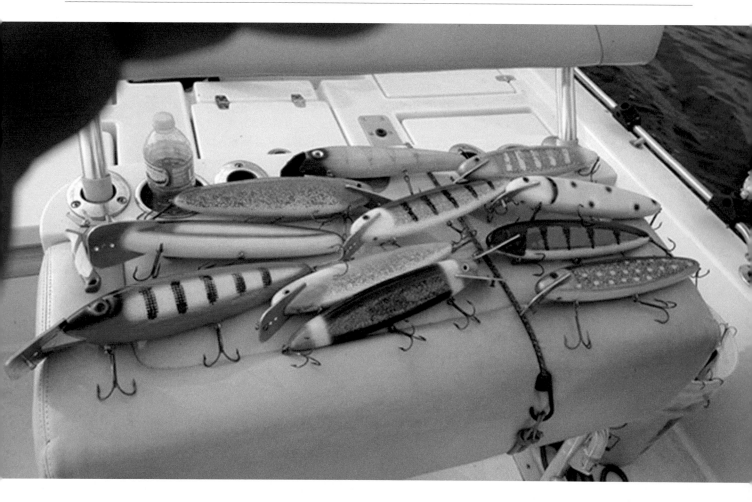

The midlake deep gravel and mud bars offer a lot of food this time of year. The walleyes flock to these areas to feed in the evenings and overnight. This is not the only place to catch fish, but when you're on the fish and nowhere on the big open water expanses of Mille Lacs is a better place to be. The bite can be nothing short of spectacular. This is one of those periods of the evening when I don't wonder if we're going to catch a lot of fish or if we will get a big one. It is more like getting ready to try and keep count and wondering how big the biggest will be.

The tactic is simple: a live bait bobber rig with a light jig tipped with a large leech. One of the keys to my success is that I never anchor my boat. The last boat I purchased was bought in 2014, and it has *never* been anchored. Instead I hold the boat with my bow-mount trolling motor's "hover" feature and slowly work my way around a structure, staying on active fish.

This is an evening where we can do no wrong. One fish here and one fish there turned into a plethora of doubles and triples, with big fish and little fish and three-pounders being about the average.

With a fish in one hand, I net another and, in a single motion, bait another jig for replacement. We get fish after fish. Everyone on the boat is up and running around and laughing. Good times! The biggest this evening is a 27.5 incher, with seventy-nine fish in a little over two hours for three fishermen.

We take sunset walleye photos and father-and-son double big fish photos. There is slime all over the floor. There are bobbers and tackle everywhere, and the boat is a mess. We button everything up, and off to shore we go. It has been another fantastic guide trip with happy customers!

At the landing, we exchange the last stories and pictures of the day. The clients' gear is unloaded and safely stored back in their vehicle, and they go on their way. But the evening is not over for the guide. After engaging in some fishing and lake conversation with other boat ramp users, I can focus back on my tasks.

Once the boat is safely back on the trailer and home, the boat needs to be cleaned. The gear needs to be put away in its proper placement on the boat, and used-up or broken gear and line are replaced. All rods are checked and retied. The cooler is cleaned out. The bait is cleaned and returned to the fridge. Everything is prepared the night before for the next morning's trips. After I talk with the morning customers, lunches are made. The cooler is restocked and packed with ice. Personal stuff is attended to, and I have a little bit to eat. The next thing I know, it's late and time for bed.

***

It is morning. The routine starts over again, but today is a little different. See, when I book half-day trips, I like to double book them. So today I have a morning half-day with one set of customers and an evening guide trip with another set. This is a common practice for me throughout the summer. This morning I meet my first customer at the gas station and buy my usual—coffee, a pickle, and a breakfast sandwich of some sort. The customers are there, and off we go to the ramp. This morning, I have a young couple and the wife's father. Today we are bass fishing!

It is a foggy start to the morning, and the boat ramp is relatively quiet. The DNR Invasive Species intern is at the ramp to educate us all on proper weed and water removal from the boat. I happen to see this young man very regularly. We chat briefly about fishing, and he asks me his DNR survey questions as I prepare the boat. The clients are all loaded, and off into the damp fog we go.

The lake is still and very quiet. We pull into a shallow rock/sand transition area, and not a sound can be heard. Off in the distance, I can here two guys talking on the shore. "Feels like a top water or jerk bait morning," I mutter.

We start the day off with a swim bait, jerk bait, and prop-style top-water bait combo for the three anglers. Right off the bat, wham! The swim bait is hooked up, and we land a giant walleye. Shortly thereafter, a large smallmouth hits the top water, and another fish hits the top water. Soon enough it's an all-out battle between Team Whopper Plopper, Team Zara Spook, and Team XRap! We hit two different locations that morning, both with the same results! There are lots of fish and decent top-water action all morning. Consistent action with explosive strikes has kept everyone aboard very entertained!

Things slow down a bit as the morning moves to afternoon. We catch a few fish on hair jigs, swim baits, and twister tails, jumping from spot to spot and working the southeast-end rocks. It is a great way to wind down a fun, fast-paced morning top-water bite on Mille Lacs Lake. We end our trip working some drop-shot rigs, learning a new technique that the customers had asked for information on. We catch a couple of little fish and a rock bass and one big walleye to end our day, with a short drop-shot-on-the-water learning session. Photos are taken. We have lots of fish, with a couple in that mid-four-pound range for our big fish of the day. Back to a very busy boat ramp we go.

When we hit the ramp, we do the usual swap of pictures and stories. The ramp is busy, with boats tied to both docks and two trailers in the water either loading or unloading. It's Saturday afternoon on a beautiful weekend here at Mille Lacs. A couple of young anglers engage me in fishing/lake conversation (this seems to happen a lot) while I get the boat loaded and ready for the road.

I go back to the homesite for an unloading and reloading of gear. Tonight we walleye fish! The boat is picked up, and gear is restocked. The cooler is repacked and filled with ice. We're going walleye fishing, so I prepare the live bait.

This midday break also makes for a great time to catch up on voice mails, customer calls, questions, emails, etc. There is always something to do in the summer, preparation-wise, for a busy fishing guide.

The next group will be met. The boat will be launched. Fish will be caught. Pictures will be taken. Slimy high fives will be given, and fish stories will be told. Then sleep will follow. On Sunday, another full-day guide trip will start right away in the morning. This is the weekend schedule of a busy guide.

CHAPTER 4

Guiding Mille Lacs

Fishing guides are a different breed. They eat, sleep, and live for fishing. Their hygiene is questionable. They know how to tie knots, sharpen hooks, clean fish, and navigate waterways, but as a group, they're pretty rough around the edges.

Most could use a haircut, a shower, and some clean clothes. Don't get me wrong; they're great people with epic knowledge. They're just not culture vultures or, as they call Twin Cities people, 612-ers (prefix of their phone number). Locals call metro people "citiots." They find the trailer-backing techniques of these city folk both funny and frustrating.

Mille Lacs has its share of guide characters—Treno, Jeff Hanson, Mike Christensen, Tim Chapman, Dave Estrem, Bill Lundeen, Tim Ajax, Tony Roach, Mark Schutz, and many more. All are great guides.

What they all have in common is that they want to be number 1 and put their customers on fish. They all have their techniques and approaches, from pulling crank baits to Lindy Rigging to slip-bobber bombing to planer boarding and more. They also sport some damn fine boats.

Who is the oddball in the group? That's Treno! He uses a 2014 Pathfinder Florida Keys boat.

Boat aside, Treno is near the top, in my opinion. He's fun, organized, patient, and knows how to catch fish. It's why I always request him for an important fishing trip or fishing tournament.

His personal record catches prove his prowess on Mille Lacs:

- Walleye, 31.5 inches
- Smallmouth bass, 23.75 inches
- Muskie, 54 inches

Great Lakes King Salmon

CHAPTER 5

Wins, Losses, and Ties

Military Appreciation Tourney (2014)

Wehking and Treno have paired up to fish Mille Lacs Lake on many memorable occasions. The most famous was the Military Appreciation Walleye Tourney hosted by Fisherman's Wharf out of Isle. In those events, the duo consistently placed near the top of the leaderboard, but they never could win it all.

The 2014 event looked like a breakthrough.

In June 2014, Treno thought they'd hit pay dirt. Wehking pulled a monster 28-inch walleye off the deep gravel flats as the 3:00 p.m. tourney expiration was about to expire. It was their fourth keeper, and both were sure they'd won their first tournament. After boating the lunker amid cheering, high fives, and fist pumps, Treno measured the fish on the walleye ruler. It just squeezed to 28 inches, a lawful keeper by Minnesota Department of Natural Resources (DNR) standards.

Treno throttled his Yamaha 150, and the powder-blue fiberglass skeeter shot out of the water, en route to the east-side resort, some ten miles away. Something strange happened as those fish banged around that live well.

Upon reaching the weigh-in, Wehking got the fish out of the box while Treno tended to a pressing full bladder. At the dock, Wehking presented the fish for weigh-in. The monster walleye looked like a game changer and gold-medal winner. But wait. The judges ruled that it only measured 27 ¾ inches. It was disqualified, sending Team Wehking-Treno to eighth place.

Treno was mortified. He was certain the fish measured 28 inches, and he figured the judges didn't properly pinch the tail and firmly press the fish down on the measuring stick. What could have been had he only been at the weigh-in. Instead the two landed the boat, hit the bar for beers and pull tabs, and agreed that someday the Military Appreciation Tourney would be theirs.

They've never won it.

Cabela's National Walleye Tournament (2015)

Treno and I are Minnesota Vikings fans. With our lake as a catch-and-release-only area, the big walleye tournaments have bypassed Mille Lacs. Much to our chagrin, Green Bay was the site of the Cabela's National Walleye Tour finals in 2015.

Treno and I qualified after winning our Mille Lacs four-team fishing league. We nudged out league organizer Michael Walters and his dad, Dave, in early August, earning a berth in the two-hundred-team national event.

With my GMC Sierra and Treno's Pathfinder in tow, we went to cheesehead country for a prefishing event, followed by the three-day tournament. Let's just say we did okay despite being outgunned by the world's best Ranger boats and guys sporting custom fishing outfits, many of them longtime anglers of the fishery in Green Bay.

We placed like seventy-first, but we wouldn't trade the experience for anything. As fishing buddies go, our dynamics are pretty simple. I make lunch, buy food, and pay for lodging and entry fees, and Treno provides the boat, bait, gear, and expertise. I come out way ahead.

As we left Green Bay, we vowed to return someday, the result of our placing on the National Walleye Tour. We hope that dream can be lived soon. With our book, we're looking at new boats now! Keep a tight line and catch a Mille Lacs monster!

Father-Son Victory

The day was likany other day. I met my customers on the dock at about 7:00 a.m. They were a father and son, with the son being about twelve years old. The boy, Charlie, was interested in fishing a little but was not totally sure yet. The dad, James, was a big fisherman and very excited to be spending a long weekend on this fishing trip with Charlie.

We started the day walleye fishing, doing a little bobber fishing and jigging. After some short instructions, Charlie had his first fish of the day—a nice, perfect eater-sized sixteen-inch walleye. I soon found out that was his first walleye ever! I hadn't picked up on the fact that Mr. Charlie had only caught panfish and largemouth bass before.

Closer to afternoon, we had switched gear and were looking for northern pike. James was working a jerk bait and had caught a little pike and a rather large walleye. Right before we broke for lunch, Charlie yelled, "I got one!" Sure enough, after a short, hard battle, I slipped the net under a nice thirty-five-inch northern pike with a crappie-colored CJ spinner in his mouth. It was not a giant but a beautiful ten-pound northern and Charlie's very first northern pike.

We broke for lunch, and afterward the guys decided that the pike sure was exciting and that they wanted to continue fishing for them. We pulled into a nearby weed edge and continued to cast (Charlie still with his lucky CJ bait).

About fifteen minutes in, I was standing up on the front bow with Charlie watching his bait, and out of nowhere, a musky came screaming out of the cabbage and smoked Charlie's lure! The fish darted under the boat, screaming drag as James was yelling, *"Muskie!"* Back around the bow, the fish surfaced and thrashed back and forth.

The battle was soon over, and with the fish in the net, we could see she had crushed the CJ. It was totally gone, and there was nothing but leader hanging out of the fish's mouth. Stretching forty-two inches, again it was not a monster but a fantastic first muskie! "What a day" was the talk of the boat. There were so many firsts for this young man; what a legendary day! I jokingly said, "Hey, what else haven't you caught?" Before I could even finish the sentence, they both shouted, "Smallmouth!"

Okay, game on. Now we hadn't planned on fishing smallmouth today. But I had my walleye gear. I rigged Charlie up a Kalin's 4-inch grub on a ¼-inch mushroom head, and with some quick instructing, Charlie was working his rig over a nice, shallow boulder pile. I knew there were fish here, but they were making him work for it.

We had a deadline. You see, the mom and the sister were waiting for dinner with the boys and were already calling. The pressure was on. No sooner than the dad said, "We better get going," Charlie set the hook! The bass came straight up out of the water, cartwheeling, trying to throw the bait.

She darted up and down and jumped multiple more times before she hit the bottom of the net! I don't think there was a boat on all of Mille Lacs' 132,000 acres that didn't hear the guys yelling! There were so many high fives and pictures throughout the day. It was an epic day for this young angler, surely one both he and his father would not soon forget. I knew for a fact that the guide would not. Write about your fire here.

Brandon's Epic Day

It was a cold early November afternoon on Mille Lacs. Today I had a trip with a good customer of mine, Brandon. Brandon is an avid fisherman who has developed a passion for muskie fishing. The plan for the day was a little casting but mostly trolling for muskie.

It was a cold and somewhat windy day on the big lake. We hadn't seen much casting and had made the commitment to troll for the rest of the day. We were following a school of tullibee on a secondary break line on a giant midlake rock structure known for being a popular fall spawning area for the tullibee.

Giant Mille Lacs muskies are always there waiting and hungry for these oily fish I like to refer to as the double cheeseburgers of Mille Lacs. We were trolling big baits today, switching between a nice mix of Supernatural MattLocks and drifters and fourteen-inch Jakes. With the sonar loaded with baitfish, we worked my trolling patterns.

About forty-five minutes into the troll, rod number 2 went off on the port side of the boat. With the rod pumping and the line clicker on the trolling reel screaming, I started yelling, *"Fish, fish!"* Brandon jumped into action and had the rod out and up within seconds! The fish surfaced right away, as most muskies do when caught trolling, and shook violent huge headshakes.

Even though a long ways from the boat, I could tell this was a special fish. An epic battle ensued. It went up and down with humongous headshakes, and then the fish stayed down deep. After a short stalemate, the fish gave in and slid across the top of the water into the bottom of the net.

The fish was a giant almost-pale Mille Lacs Lake beast of a muskie! Measurements put the fish at fifty-three inches long with a twenty-seven-inch girth; it was a fifty-pound supertanker!

Brandon had just landed his second muskie ever, and it happened to be a fish that would make even the most seasoned muskie angler jealous! "People musky fish entire lifetimes searching for a fish like that."

We trolled for the remainder of the evening and had another large fish hooked up that unfortunately came unbuttoned. It didn't matter. The talk in the boat was 100 percent focused on Brandon's fish of a lifetime!

Mike and Bridget Win!

Mike and Bridget were a young couple and avid walleye fishermen out for an evening of walleye fishing with me. It was a beautiful, flat, calm late June afternoon/evening as we were pulling away from Izaty's Marina on the south shores of Mille Lacs.

We had been bouncing around, bobber fishing walleyes, and were doing well. We were not setting any lake records, but the fish were biting and good times were being had. With each spot change, we ventured farther and farther out from the southern shoreline. And it seemed like with each move, the fish started biting better.

I made once last boat ride out and said to Mike that we were ending the evening on one of my best big-fish spots. We were on a deep mudflat that, on one particular inside turn, seemed to always kick me a big fish.

Mike and I were sitting in the back of the boat chatting, and Bridget was up on the bow all by herself, fishing away. I heard a shuffling up front and turned around, and Bridget's fishing rod was bent clear down to the handle.

Laughingly, I joked, "Hey, you got one." Up and down, the fish just would not leave the bottom. It was literally right below our feet yet still thirty-two feet away! Bridget was fighting the fish beautifully and soon started to pull the fish closer to the surface. When it was about two-thirds of the way up, I could see the walleye, and it was a dandy! The fish made another run straight to the bottom.

Not wanting to startle or jinx it, I said nothing more than "You're doing a great job! That's a nice fish!" I knew this would go down as one of the biggest walleyes of the season. Finally, the fish was tiring and coming up.

As the fish hit the surface and I scooped it with the net, I heard Mike from the back. "Holy cow, that's a giant." Bam! It was a giant 30.5-inch Mille Lacs Lake walleye! There was laughter, high fives, and hugs all around the boat! We had a very long bug-filled ride back to the marina. There were lots of bug-filled smiles when we hit the dock!

CHAPTER 6

Tools

Tools

Boat: 22.5-foot Pathfinder TRS 2200
Motor: Yamaha 150 Outboard
Graphs: Lowrance, Hummingbird
Rods: St. Croix and Thorne Brothers
Reels: Shimano

Gear –

Preferred equipment for Matt Treno includes Thorne Bros. custom and St Croix rods. For reels Matt uses mostly Shimano but has a nice mix of Daiwa reels. Suffix 832 and Power Pro for braided light lines and Cortland Masterbraid bronze back 80 lb for muskies. Sunline and Seaguar round out his fluorocarbon choices. Matt always says "I burn through about a billion yards of Trilene XL clear in 6lb a season" when it comes to a mono line.

It's hard to miss Matt Treno in his 22 foot Pathfinder center counsel bay boat. Matt loves the open layout and huge decks that this boat provides and of course how it handles the big water Mille Lacs is known to have. "This boat can handle a lot more than anybody would ever want to be out in" Matt always says. When asked about motors Matt can never say enough good things about his Yamaha four stroke motor. "The main thing is the motor has to start every time no matter what". Matt also enjoys the great fuel economy the motor provides.

Treno's Pathfinder Guide Boat

EPILOGUE

It took years of guiding, catching, and taking photos for the material for this book. Matt and I wrote this in a little over one week. We put in some long nights and some very early mornings. We hope you enjoy it. It was launched with hopes that it would be available for the May 11 Minnesota fishing opener. We're sure it'll make for an epic Father's Day or Christmas gift.

From those I have talked to and from what I have read, with the number of hours Treno logs on Mille Lacs, who better has a chance to break those state records?

I think we'll see at least one of them broken by Treno this 2018 season. Until then, keep a tight line, get a fishing license, and come share your lunker stories at Izaty's Resort or Bayview Bar and Grill on mighty Mille Lacs' south central shore.

ABOUT THE AUTHORS

Michael Wehking

Michael Wehking has recently authored nine books. The first eight focus on winning casino table gaming and are published by Xlibris. He's a retired army major who now splits time between Arizona and Minnesota. Can you guess where he spends winters and summers? He's an avid six-handicap golfer and fisherman with a recent penchant for world travel. He's married to his wife, Kathy, and has three adult children—Rachel, Kyle, and Eric (Amber).

Wehking graduated from St. Cloud State University, where he was a mass communication major in the news editorial program. He credits SCSU professors Michael Vadnie and J. Brent Norlem for solid training and writing courses and internships. He especially credits Dave DeLand, Mike Killeen, Tom Elliott, and Kevin Oklobzija as mentors who coached him through a three-year stint as a part-time sports writer at the *St. Cloud Times*.

After serving twenty-four years in the army, Wehking retired and ran a social media Mille Lacs marketing website. He has mowed the pristine shoreline at Izaty's on the south shore of Mille Lacs Lake for the last ten years. In November, he launched his poker table gaming career.

Matt Treno

Treno has been a multispecies fishing guide on Mille Lacs Lake for just over a decade. Treno spent many seasons as a launch captain for multiple resorts. Treno still maintains his Minnesota captain's license just in case he has time to drive a launch or two throughout the summer.

Fishing these waters since he was a boy, Treno got his start in the Twin Cities area after graduating from Edina High School. After high school, Treno traveled around and bounced between jobs before landing in the

real estate world. Matt excelled in this world and was well on his way to a very successful career. But it just wasn't his calling. Soon his passions got control of him, and he decided to make the move north.

Upon moving north to the Mille Lacs area, he wasn't sure where his path would take him. Treno knew he wanted to fish daily and had a calling to this big lake he had fished for so many years. During the summer of 200, Treno was asked to take a job as a guide. One job turned into two, and soon after, MattsFishing.com was born. Although Treno's quest was met with a lot of local and family resistance, he knew after those first few guide trips that he had found his calling.

Treno says that getting his feet wet and getting his business up and running took a lot of long hours and hard work. Certainly he was met with local roadblocks. He has enjoyed many ups and downs with different species throughout his seasons at this great lake. Times have changed a lot over his still relatively young fishing career. One thing Treno has always taken pride in is that no matter how hard the fishing gets, he stays focused. Keeping your head down, working hard, and producing results will get you to the top.

Printed in the United States
By Bookmasters